The Thank You Book

The Thank You Book

Story by Carole Stuart

Illustrated by Arthur Robins

Four Walls Eight Windows
New York/London

Text copyright © 2001 Lyle Stuart
Illustration copyright © 2001 Arthur Robins

Published in the United States by
Four Walls Eight Windows
39 West 14th Street
New York, NY 10011
http://www.4w8w.com

UK offices:
Four Walls Eight Windows/Turnaround
Unit 3 Olympia Trading Estate
Coburg Road, Wood Green
London N22 6TZ

First printing April 2001.

All rights reserved. No part of this book may be reproduced, stored in a database or other retrieval system, or transmitted in any form, by any means, including mechanical, electronic, photocopying, recording, or otherwise, without the prior written permission of the publisher.

Library of Congress Cataloging-in-Publication Data:
Stuart, Carole
The thank you book / by Carole Stuart ; illustrated by Arthur Robins.
p. cm.
ISBN: 1-56858-170-X (hardcover)
1. Etiquette for children and teenagers. [1. Etiquette.] I. Robins, Arthur, ill. II. Title.

BJ1857.C5 S85 2001
395.1'22--dc21   00-067193

Printed in Hong Kong

10   9   8   7   6   5   4   3   2   1

Psst!

Would you like to learn two extra-special, extra-ordinary, extra-amazing magic words?

Now these MAGIC words won't turn your living room carpet into a space cadet's racing pod.

And they won't mysteriously—Poof!—transform a plate full of cauliflower into a candy bar.

But they aren't silly words that are hard to remember either like poofywinkle or snifflejerky.

Nope. These two magic words are *thank you*.
    Yes—*thank* and *you*.

So what makes them magic?

Well, when you say them to another person, you make that person feel really nice. You make that person think, "Hey, I'm glad I did something for this kid." And you've let them know you're glad they did something for you.

Now you may be saying to yourself, "Sure, when Grandpa gives me that cool game, yes, yes, yes, yes, absolutely yes, of course, I say thank you, thank you, thank you!!!!" But UPS doesn't deliver presents like that every day of the week.

You know what, though? There are many, many things, big and small, that people do for you every day that call for a big loud thank you.

12

Each morning when you wake up, you have inside a fresh supply of thank yous. You can hand them out to people as if they were beautiful flowers or Tootsie Roll Lollypops.

How about when you're late for school and you grab your coat and backpack as you head for the door.

Rounding the corner for the front hall, you catch a glimpse of yourself in the mirror. Your hair is sticking up like porcupine quills. Aargh! But, don't worry, it's Dad to the rescue. He offers to give you a ride to school and the use of his comb. Wouldn't this be a good time for a thank you?

Sure would.

Now you're working hard in school trying to cut out the perfect star. A snip here. A snip there. Another snip. Nope. The star is still crooked. Your teacher, Mrs. No-nonsense, sees your problem and says, "Why don't you try a little cut here?" Suddenly the star is perfect.

A thank you from you magically brings a smile to Mrs. No-nonsense's face.

"Wow, this child has good manners," she thinks.

Finally, it's lunch time. Peanut butter and jelly. But, it's just not a peanut butter-and-jelly kind of day. Patooie, you wish you had something else.

Then Ahmed, the new kid in your class, says he has turkey and cheese, but he loves peanut butter, especially with jelly.

"Do you want to switch?" Ahmed asks.

"Hey, thanks, Ahmed."

"No, thank you."

And you both feel good.

School's over, and you're walking home. There's that one busy street to cross. You'd be scared except that the crossing guard who looks like Mother Goose is there with her big yellow and red sign. When she holds it up, cars, minivans, and even big trucks come to a complete stop. She doesn't put the sign down until you're safely on the other side.

A loud thank you will make that crossing guard happy she helped.

When Mom comes home, she asks if everyone would like to go out for a pizza.

Yummy, cheesy pizza! Your favorite!

"Yes, yes, thank you."

Later, when everyone says, "thank you," Mom says, "Hey, maybe I should suggest this more often."

You're ready first, so you help out by getting your baby sister into her shoes. This isn't easy since she likes to play with her toes.

Guess what happens then?
Dad and Mom both say,
"thank you," to you.

Later when you get into bed, Dad reads you your favorite book about magic and spells. "Thanks, Dad," you say.

You can even say thank you to Stripes, your cat, when she puts her paws on your cheeks and gives you a kitty-kind-of-hug good night.

This saying thank you stuff is okay. The words don't cost you anything, but they are so good that people gobble them up like milk chocolate candies and vanilla ice-cream cones.

And there are always more inside you that you can give away to someone who does something nice.

Even if you live in another country, you can say thank you.

In Egypt, where Ahmed's family came from, they say *shukran*. In France they say *merci*. People who speak Spanish say *gracias*.

It's *danke schön* in Germany and *grazie* in Italy. And in Japan they say *arigato*.

As you drift off to sleep to dream of wizards and wonders, Mom and Dad kiss your forehead and whisper, "Thank you for being you."

Thinking a thank you doesn't count. No one can hear a thank you that stays in your head. So remember to say it out loud.

You'll make everyone feel good . . . and you'll feel good, too!

And thank you for reading this book!